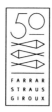

FARRAR
STRAUS
GIROUX

Lies

I Am the Bitter Name

With Ignorance

Sophocles' Women of Trachis (with Gregory Dickerson)

The Lark. The Thrush. The Starling. (Poems from Issa)

Tar

Flesh and Blood

Poems 1963–1983

The Bacchae of Euripides

A Dream of Mind

Selected Poems

The Vigil

THE VIGIL

THE

VIGIL

C. K. Williams

Farrar, Straus and Giroux

New York

Library of Congress Cataloging-in-Publication Data
Williams, C. K. (Charles Kenneth).
    The vigil : poems / C. K. Williams. — 1st ed.
        p.   cm.
    ISBN 0-374-22653-9 (alk. paper)
    I. Title.
    PS3573.I4483V54   1997
    811'.54—dc20
    96-17253
    CIP

Some of these poems have been published previously, some of them in
different forms: "Dominion: Depression," "My Fly," "Hercules, Deianira,
Nessus," "Time: 1976," "Secrets," "My Book, My Book," "Time: 1978,"
"The Game," "Spider Psyche" and "Villanelle of the Suicide's Mother"
in Selected Poems; "The Neighbor" in The New Yorker; *"Fragment" in*
Slate; *"The Hovel," "The Coma" and "Hawk" in* Agni Review; *"Proof"*
in The New Republic; *"Time: 1975," "The Bed" and "The Heart" in*
Ontario Review; *"Cave," "Symbols: Wind, Guitar, Owl, Dog, Fire,*
Dawn, Wig, Garden," "Realms," "Money," "Song," "In Darkness" and
"Grace" in The American Poetry Review; *"Grief" in* DoubleTake *and*
American Poetry Review; *"Realms" (under the title "The Vigil"), "Song"*
and "Exterior: Day" in The Times Literary Supplement; *"Storm" in*
The Progressive; *"The Lover" in* Michigan Quarterly Review; *"Insight"*
in Threepenny Review; *and "Old Man" in* The Yale Review.

for Catherine, always

CONTENTS

I

The Neighbor, 3

Dominion: Depression, 6

Fragment, 8

The Hovel, 9

My Fly, 10

Hercules, Deianira, Nessus, 12

Instinct, 15

Time: 1976, 16

The Coma, 18

Proof, 20

Secrets, 21

The Widower, 24

Money, 25

My Book, My Book, 26

Time: 1975, 27

Cave, 28

Grief, 29

II

Symbols

1 / WIND, 35

2 / GUITAR, 36

3 / OWL, 37

4 / DOG, 38

5 / FIRE, 39

6 / DAWN, 40

7 / WIG, 41

8 / GARDEN, 42

III

Realms, 45

Storm, 47

Song, 49

Insight, 50

In Darkness, 55

The Demagogue, 57

The Bed, 58

The Heart, 60

Exterior: Day, 61

Time: 1978, 62

Hawk, 64

The Lover, 66

The Game, 67

Spider Psyche, 68

Grace, 70

Time: 1972, 72

Villanelle of the Suicide's Mother, 73

Thirst, 74

Old Man, 76

I

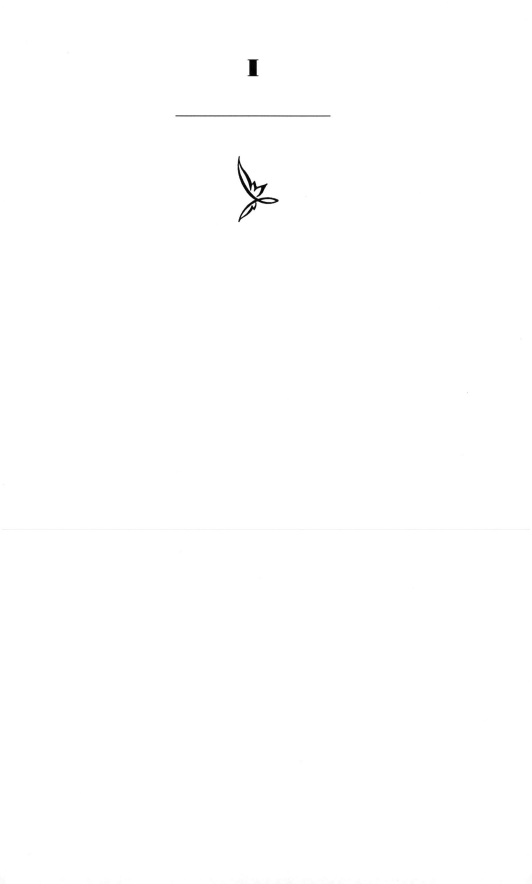

The Neighbor

Her five horrid, deformed little dogs, who incessantly yap on the roof
    under my window;
her cats, god knows how many, who must piss on her rugs—her landing's
    a sickening reek;
her shadow, once, fumbling the chain on her door, then the door slam-
    ming fearfully shut:
only the barking, and the music, jazz, filtering as it does day and night
    into the hall.

The time it was Chris Conner singing "Lush Life," how it brought back
    my college sweetheart,
my first real love, who, till I left her, played the same record, and, head
    on my shoulder,
hand on my thigh, sang sweetly along, of regrets and depletions she was
    too young for,
as I was too young, later, to believe in her pain: it startled, then bored,
    then repelled me.

My starting to fancy she'd ended up in this firetrap in the Village, that
    my neighbor was her;
my thinking we'd meet, recognize one another, become friends, that I'd
    accomplish a penance;
my seeing her—it wasn't her—at the mailbox, grey-yellow hair, army
    pants under a nightgown:
her turning away, hiding her ravaged face in her hands, muttering an
    inappropriate "Hi."

Sometimes, there are frightening goings-on in the stairwell, a man shout-
    ing *Shut up!*

the dogs frantically snarling, claws scrabbling, then her, her voice, hoarse, harsh, hollow,
almost only a tone, incoherent, a note, a squawk, bone on metal, metal gone molten,
calling them back, Come back, darlings; come back, dear ones, my sweet angels, come back.

Medea she was, next time I saw her, sorceress, tranced, ecstatic, stock-still on the sidewalk,
ragged coat hanging agape, passersby flowing around her, her mouth torn suddenly open,
as though in a scream, silently though, as though only in her brain or breast had it erupted:
a cry so pure, practiced, detached, it had no need of a voice or could no longer bear one.

These invisible links that allure, these transfigurations even of anguish that hold us:
the girl, my old love, the last, lost time I saw her, when she came to find me at a party:
her drunkenly stumbling, falling, sprawling, skirt hiked, eyes veined red, swollen with tears;
her shame, her dishonor; my ignorant, arrogant coarseness; my secret pride, my turning away.

Still life on a roof top: dead trees in barrels, a bench, broken; dogs, excrement, sky.
What pathways through pain, what junctures of vulnerability, what crossings and counterings?

Too many lives in our lives already, too many chances for sorrow, too
    many unaccounted-for pasts.
Behold me, the god of frenzied, inexhaustible love says, rising in bloody
    splendor: *Behold me!*

Her making her way down the littered vestibule stairs, one agonized step
    at a time;
my holding the door, her crossing the fragmented tiles, faltering at the
    step to the street,
droning, not looking at me, "Can you help me?" taking my arm, leaning
    lightly against me;
her wavering step into the world, her whispering, "Thanks, love," lightly,
    lightly against me.

Dominion: Depression

I don't know what day or year of their secret cycle this blazing golden
    afternoon might be,
but out in the field in a shrub hundreds of pairs of locusts are locked
    in a slow sexual seizure.

Hardly more animate than the few leaves they haven't devoured, they
    seethe like a single being,
limbs, antennas, and wings all tangled together as intricately as a layer
    of neurons.

Always the neat, tight, gazeless helmet, the exoskeleton burnished like
    half-hardened glue;
always the abdomen twitched deftly under or aside, the skilled rider, the
    skillfully ridden.

One male, though, has somehow severed a leg, it sways on the spike of
    a twig like a harp:
he lunges after his female, tilts, falls; the mass horribly shudders, shifts,
    realigns.

So dense, so hard, so immersed in their terrible need to endure, so
    unlike me but like me,
why do they seem such a denial, why do I feel if I plunged my hand
    in among them I'd die?

This must be what god thinks, beholding his ignorant, obstinate, libid-
    inally maniacal offspring:
wanting to stop them, to keep them from being so much an image of
    his impotence or his will.

How divided he is from his creation: even here near the end he sees
       moving towards him
a smaller, sharper, still more gleaming something, extracting moist mat-
       ter from a skull.

No more now: he waits, fists full of that mute, oily, crackling, crystalline
       broil,
then he feels at last the cool wingbeat of the innocent void moving in
       again over the world.

Fragment

This time the hold up man didn't know a video-sound camera hidden
    up in a corner
was recording what was before it or more likely he didn't care, opening
    up with his pistol,
not saying a word, on the clerk you see blurredly falling and you hear
    —I keep hearing—
crying, "God! God!" in that voice I was always afraid existed within us,
    the voice that knows
beyond illusion the irrevocability of death, beyond any dream of being
    not mortally injured—
"You're just going to sleep, someone will save you, you'll wake again,
    loved ones beside you . . ."
Nothing of that: even torn by the flaws in the tape it was a voice that
    knew it was dying,
knew it was being—horrible—slaughtered, all that it knew and aspired
    to instantly voided;
such hopeless, astonished pleading, such overwhelmed, untempered pity
    for the self dying;
no indignation, no passion for justice, only woe, woe, woe, as he felt
    himself falling,
even falling knowing already he was dead, and how much I pray to
    myself I want not, ever,
to know this, how much I want to ask why I must, with such perfect,
    detailed precision,
know this, this anguish, this agony for a self departing wishing only to
    stay, to endure,
knowing all the while that, having known, I always will know this torn,
    singular voice
of a soul calling "God!" as it sinks back through the darkness it came
    from, cancelled, annulled.

The Hovel

Slate scraps, split stone, third hand splintering timber; rusted nails and
    sheet-tin;
dirt floor, chinks the wind seeps through, the stink of an open sewer
    streaming behind;
rags, flies, stench, and never, it seems, clear air, light, a breeze of be-
    nevolent clemency.

My hut, my home, the destiny only deferred of which all I live now is
    deflection, illusion:
war, plunder, pogrom; crops charred, wife ravished, children starved,
    stolen, enslaved;
muck, toil, hunger, never a moment for awareness, of bird song, of
    dawn's immaculate stillness.

Back bent, knees shattered, teeth rotting; fever and lesion, the physical
    knowledge of evil;
illiterate, numb, insensible, superstitious, lurching from lust to hunger
    to unnameable dread:
the true history I inhabit, its sea of suffering, its wave to which I am
    froth, scum.

My Fly

for Erving Goffman, 1922–1982

One of those great, garishly emerald flies that always look freshly gen-
    erated from fresh excrement
and who maneuver through our airspace with a deft intentionality that
    makes them seem to think,
materializes just above my desk, then vanishes, his dense, abrasive buzz
    sucked in after him.

I wait, imagine him, hidden somewhere, waiting, too, then think, who
    knows why, of you—
don't laugh—that he's a messenger from you, or that you yourself (you'd
    howl at this),
ten years afterwards have let yourself be incarnated as this pestering anti-
    angel.

Now he, or you, abruptly reappears, with a weightless pounce alighting
    near my hand.
I lean down close, and though he has to sense my looming presence,
    he patiently attends,
as though my study of him had become an element of his own
    observations—maybe it is you!

Joy! To be together, even for a time! Yes, tilt your fuselage, turn it
    towards the light,
aim the thousand lenses of your eyes back up at me: how I've missed
    the layers of your attention,
how often been bereft without your gift for sniffing out pretentiousness
    and moral sham.

Why would you come back, though? Was that other radiance not intri-
    cate enough to parse?

Did you find yourself in some monotonous century hovering down the
    tidy queue of creatures
waiting to experience again the eternally unlikely bliss of being matter
    and extension?

You lift, you land—you're rushed, I know; the interval in all our ter-
    minals is much too short.
Now you hurl against the window, skid and jitter on the pane: I open
    it and step aside
and follow for one final moment of felicity your brilliant ardent atom
    swerving through.

Hercules, Deianira, Nessus

from Ovid, Metamorphoses, Book IX

There was absolutely no reason after the centaur had pawed her and
 tried to mount her,
after Hercules waiting across the raging river for the creature to carry
 her to him
heard her cry out and launched an arrow soaked in the hydra's incurable
 venom into the monster,
that Deianira should have believed him, Nessus, horrible thing, as he
 died but she did.

We see the end of the story: Deianira anguished, aghast, suicide-sword
 in her hand;
Hercules' blood hissing and seething like water in which molten rods
 are plunged to anneal,
but how could a just-married girl hardly out of her father's house have
 envisioned all that,
and even conjecturing that Nessus was lying, plotting revenge, how
 could she have been sure?

We see the centaur as cunning, malignant, a hybrid from the savage
 time before ours
when emotion always was passion and passion was always unchecked by
 commandment or conscience;
she sees only a man-horse, mortally hurt, suddenly harmless, eyes sud-
 denly soft as a foal's,
telling her, "Don't be afraid, come closer, listen": offering homage,
 friendship, a favor.

In our age of scrutiny and dissection we know Deianira's mind better
 than she does herself:

we know the fortune of women as chattel and quarry, objects to be won
        then shunted aside;
we understand the cost of repression, the repercussions of unsatisfied
        rage and resentment,
but consciousness then was still new, Deianira inhabited hers like the
        light from a fire.

Or might she have glimpsed with that mantic prescience the gods hadn't
        yet taken away
her hero a lifetime later on the way home with another king's daughter,
        callow, but lovely,
lovely enough to erase from Hercules' scruples not only his vows but
        the simple convention
that tells you you don't bring a rival into your aging wife's weary, sor-
        rowful bed?

. . . No, more likely the centaur's promise intrigued in itself: an infallible
        potion of love.
"Just gather the clots of blood from my wound: here, use my shirt, then
        hide it away.
Though so exalted, so regal a woman as you never would need it, it
        might still be of use:
whoever's shoulders it touches, no matter when, will helplessly, hope-
        lessly love you forever."

See Hercules now in the shirt Deianira has sent him approaching the
        fire of an altar,
the garment suddenly clinging, the hydra, his long-vanquished foe, alive
        in its threads,

each thread a tentacle clutching at him, each chemical tentacle acid,
adhering, consuming,
charring before his horrified eyes skin from muscle, muscle from ten-
don, tendon from bone.

Now Deianira, back then, the viscous gouts of Nessus' blood dyeing her
diffident hands:
if she could imagine us watching her there in her myth, how would she
want us to see her?
Surely as symbol, a petal of sympathy caught in the perilous rift between
culture and chaos,
not as the nightmare she'd be, a corpse with a slash of tardy self-
knowledge deep in its side.

What Hercules sees as he pounds up the bank isn't himself cremated
alive on his pyre,
shrieking as Jove his Olympian father extracts his immortal essence from
its agonized sheathing—
he sees what's before him: the woman, his bride, kneeling to the dark,
rushing river,
obsessively scrubbing away, he must think, the nocuous, mingled reek
of horse, hydra, human.

14

Instinct

Although he's apparently the youngest (his little Rasta-beard is barely
    down and feathers),
most casually connected (he hardly glances at the girl he's with, though
    she might be his wife),
half-sloshed (or more than half) on picnic-whiskey teen-aged father,
    when his little son,
two or so, tumbles from the slide, hard enough to scare himself, hard
    enough to make him cry,
really cry, not partly cry, not pretend the fright for what must be some
    scarce attention,
but really let it out, let loudly be revealed the fear of having been so
    close to real fear,
he, the father, knows just how quickly he should pick the child up, then
    how firmly hold it,
fit its head into the muscled socket of his shoulder, rub its back, croon
    and whisper to it,
and finally pull away a little, about a head's length, looking, still con-
    cerned, into its eyes,
then smiling, broadly, brightly, as though something had been shared,
    something of importance,
not dreadful, or not very, not at least now that it's past, but rather some-
    thing . . . funny,
funny, yes, it was funny, wasn't it, to fall and cry like that, though one
    certainly can understand,
we've all had glimpses of a premonition of the anguish out there, you're
    better now, though,
aren't you, why don't you go back and try again, I'll watch you, maybe
    have another drink,
yes, my son, my love, I'll go back and be myself now: you go be the
    person you are, too.

Time: 1976

Time for my break; I'm walking from my study down the long hallway
    towards the living room.
Catherine is there, on the couch, reading to Jed, the phonograph is
    playing Bach's *Offering*.
I can just hear Catherine's voice as she shows Jed the pictures: *Voilà le
    château, voilà Babar,*
and with no warning I'm taken with a feeling that against all logic I
    recognize to be regret,
as violent and rending a regret as anything I've ever felt, and I under-
    stand immediately
that all of this familiar beating and blurring, the quickening breath, the
    gathering despair,
almost painful all, has to do with the moment I'm in, and my mind,
    racing to keep order,
thrusts this way and that and finally casts itself, my breath along with it,
    into the future.

2

Ten years from now, or twenty; I'm walking down the same hallway, I
    hear the same music,
the same sounds—Catherine's story, Jed's chirps of response—but I know
    with anxiety
that most of this is only in my mind: the reality is that Catherine and
    Jed are no longer there,
that I'm merely constructing this—what actually accompanies me down
    that corridor is memory:

16

here, in this tentative but terribly convincing future I think to myself
     that it must be the music—
the Bach surely is real, I can *hear* it—that drives me so poignantly,
     expectantly back
to remember again that morning of innocent peace a lifetime ago when
     I came towards them;
the sunny room, the music, the voices, each more distinct now: *Voilà
     le château, voilà Babar* . . .

3

But if I'm torn so with remembrance in *this* present, then something
     here must be lost.
Has Jed grown, already left home? Has Catherine gone on somewhere,
     too, to some other life?
But no, who'd have played the record: perhaps they, or one of them,
     either one would be enough,
will still be out there before me, not speaking, perhaps reading, looking
     out the window, waiting.
Maybe all this grief, then, was illusion; a sadness, not for loss, but for
     the nature of time:
in my already fading future, I try to find a reconciliation for one more
     imaginary absence . . .
All this, sensation, anxiety, and speculation, goes through me in an in-
     stant, then in another,
a helplessness at what mind will do, then back into the world: *Voilà
     Babar, voilà la vieille dame* . . .

17

The Coma

for the memory of S. J. Marks

"My character wound," he'd written so shortly before, "my flaw," and
     now he was dying,
his heart, his anguished heart stopping, maiming his brain, then being
     started again;
"my loneliness," in his childish square cursive, "I've been discarded but
     I've earned it,
I'd like to grow fainter and fainter then disappear; my arrogant, inau-
     thentic false self."

"My weak, hopeless, incompetent reparations," he'd written in his lone-
     liness and despair,
"there's so much I'm afraid of facing, my jealousy, my inertia; roots are
     tearing from my brain."
And now, as he lay in his coma, I thought I could hear him again, "I'm
     insensitive, ineffectual,
I seethe with impatience," hear him driving himself with the shattered
     bolt of his mind deeper,

"It's my fault, my arrogant doubt, my rage," but I hoped, imagining him
     now waking downwards,
hoped he'd believe for once in the virtues his ruined past had never let
     him believe in,
his gifts for sympathy, kindness, compassion; in the ever-ascending
     downwards of dying,
I hoped he'd know that his passion to be goodness had made him good-
     ness, like a child;

not "my malaise, my destructive neurosis": let him have known for him-
     self his purity and his warmth;

not "my crippled, hateful disdain": let have come to him, in his last lift
      away from himself,
his having wanted to heal the world he'd found so wounded in himself;
      let him have known,
though his sorrow wouldn't have wanted him to, that, in his love and
      affliction, he had.

Proof

Not to show off, but elaborating some philosophical assertion, "Watch
    her open her mouth,"
says the guardian of an elderly, well-dressed retarded woman to the little
    circle of ladies
companionably gathered under a just-flowering chestnut this lusciously
    balmy Sunday.

She moves her hand in to everyone else an imperceptible gesture, her
    charge opens wide,
a peanut, to murmurs of approbation, is inserted, though all absorbed
    again as they are,
nobody sees when a moment later it slips from the still-visible tongue
    to the lip, then falls,

the mouth staying tensely agape, as though news of a great calamity had
    just reached it,
as though in eternity's intricate silent music someone had frighteningly
    mis-struck a chord,
so everything else has to hold, too, lovers strolling, children setting boats
    out on the pond,

until the guardian takes notice and says not unkindly, "Close, dear,"
    which is dutifully done,
and it all can start over: voices, leaves, water, air; always the yearning,
    sensitive air,
urging against us, aspiring to be us, the light striking across us: signs,
    covenants, codes.

Secrets

I didn't know that the burly old man who lived in a small house like
    ours down the block in Newark
was a high-up in the mob on the docks until I was grown and my father
    finally told me.

Neither did it enter my mind until much too much later that my su-
    perior that year at Nisner's,
a dazzlingly bright black man, would never in those days climb out of
    his mindless stockroom.

The councilman on the take, the girl upstairs giving free oral sex, the
    loansharks and addicts—
it was all news to me: do people hide things from me to protect me?
    Do they mistrust me?

Even when Sid Mizraki was found beaten to death in an alley, I didn't
    hear until years later.
Sid murdered! God, my god, was all I could say. Poor, sad Sidney; poor
    hard-luck Sid!

I hadn't known Sidney that long, but I liked him: plump, awkward, he
    was gentle, eager to please,
the way unprepossessing people will be; we played ball, went to Chi-
    natown with the guys.

He'd had a bleak life: childhood in the streets, bad education, no
    women, irrelevant jobs;
in those days he worked for the city, then stopped; I had no idea of his
    true tribulations.

As the tale finally found me, Sid had a boss who hated him, rode him, drove him insane,
and Sid one drunk night in a bar bribed some burglars he knew to kill the creep for him.

I can't conceive how you'd dream up something like that, or how you'd know people like that,
but apparently Sid had access to tax rolls, and rich people's addresses he was willing to trade.

Then suddenly he was transferred, got a friendlier boss, forgot the whole witless affair,
but a year or so later the thieves were caught and as part of their plea bargain sold Sid.

He got off with probation, but was fired, of course, and who'd hire him with that record?
He worked as a bartender, went on relief, drifted, got into drugs, some small-time dealing.

Then he married—"the plainest woman on earth," someone told me— but soon was divorced:
more drugs, more dealing, run-ins with cops, then his unthinkable calvary in that alley.

It was never established who did it, or why; no one but me was surprised it had happened.
A bum found him, bleeding, broken, inert; a friend from before said, "His torments are over."

Well, Sid, what now? Shall I sing for you, celebrate you with some truth?
      Here's truth:
add up what you didn't know, friend, and I don't, and you might have
      one conscious person.

No, this has nothing to do with your omissions or sins or failed rectifi-
      cations, but mine:
to come so close to a life and not comprehend it, acknowledge it, truly
      know it is life.

How can I feel so clearly the shudder of blows, even the blessed oblivion
      breaking on you,
and not really grasp what you were in yourself to yourself, what secrets
      sustained you?

So, for once I know something, that if anyone's soul should be singing,
      Sidney, it's yours.
Poor poet, you'd tell me, *poor sheltered creature: if you can't open your
      eyes, at least stay still.*

The Widower

He'd tried for years to leave her, then only months ago he finally had;
     now she's dead,
and though he claims he hates her still, I can tell he really loves and is
     obsessed by her.
I commiserate with him about her faults, her anarchic temperament,
     her depressing indolence,
the way she'd carried on when he'd moved out, spying on him, tele-
     phoning at all hours,
until his anger moves towards malice, bitterness, and he attacks her even
     for her virtues,
her mildness, her impulsive generosity, then I don't quite disagree, it's
     too soon for that,
but I at least demur, firmly enough to alleviate my already over-
     compromised conscience
but discreetly enough to allow him to re-expound his thesis that her
     frenzied desperation
at their parting was one more proof of her neurosis, and had nothing to
     do with her dying,
which was just a cardiac, a circulation thing—how primitively Freudian
     to think otherwise—
though he and I both know, as surely as we're going on with this, on
     and on with this,
she brought about her death herself, as much as if she'd shot herself,
     and he,
because he still loved her so but found her still so impossible to love,
     as much as let her.

Money

How did money get into the soul; how did base dollars and cents ascend
    from the slime
to burrow their way into the crannies of consciousness, even it feels like
    into the flesh?

Wants with no object, needs with no end, like bacteria bringing their
    fever and freezing,
viruses gnawing at neurons, infecting even the sanctuaries of altruism
    and self-worth.

We asked soul to be huge, encompassing, sensitive, knowing, all-
    knowing, but not this,
not money roaring in with battalions of pluses and minus, setting up
    camps of profit and loss,

not joy become calculation, life counting itself, compounding itself like
    a pocket of pebbles:
sorrow, it feels like; a weeping, unhealable wound, an affront at all costs
    to be avenged.

Greed, taint and corruption, this sickness, this buy and this miserable
    sell;
soul against soul, talons of caustic tungsten: *what has been done to us,*
    what have we done?

My Book, My Book

The book goes fluttering crazily through the space of my room towards
    the wall like a bird
stunned in mid-flight and impacts and falls not like a bird but more
    brutally, like a man,
mortally sprawling, spine torn from its sutures, skeletal glue fragmented
    to crystal and dust.

Submissive, inert, it doesn't as would any other thing wounded shudder,
    quake, shiver,
act out at least desperate, reflexive attempts towards persistence, endur-
    ance, but how could it,
wasn't it shriven already of all but ambition and greed; rote, lame em-
    ulations of conviction?

. . . Arrives now to my mind the creature who'll sniff out someday what
    in this block of pretension,
what protein, what atom, might still remain to digest and abstract, trans-
    figure to gist,
what trace of life substance wasn't abraded away by the weight of its
    lovelessness and its sham.

Come, little borer, sting your way in, tunnel more deeply, blast, mine,
    excavate, drill:
take my book to you, etherealize me in the crunch of your gut; refine
    me, release me:
let me cling to your brainstem, dissolve in your dreaming: verse, page,
    quire; devour me, devourer.

Time: 1975

My father-in-law is away, Catherine and I and Renée, her mother, are
  eating in the kitchen;
Jed, three weeks old, sleeps in his floppy straw cradle on the counter
  next to the bread box;
we've just arrived, and I'm so weary with jet lag, with the labor of tend-
  ing to a newborn
that my mind drifts and, instead of their words, I listen to the music of
  the women's voices.

Some family business must be being resolved: Renée is agitated, her
  tone suddenly urgent,
there's something she's been waiting to tell; her eyes hold on Catherine's
  and it's that,
the intensity of her gaze, that brings back to me how Catherine looked
  during her labor—
all those hours—then, the image startlingly vivid, I see Renée giving
  birth to Catherine.

I see the darkened room, then the bed, then, sinews drawn tight in her
  neck, Renée herself,
with the same abstracted look in her eyes that Catherine had, layer on
  layer of self disadhering,
all the dross gone, all but the fire of concentration, the heart-stopping
  beauty, and now,
at last, my Catherine, our Catherine, here for us all, blazing, bawling,
  lacquered with gore.

Cave

Not yet a poet, not yet a person perhaps, or a human, or not so far as
    I'd know now,
I lurk in the lobe of a cave, before me sky, a tangle of branch, a tree I
    can't name.

Not yet in a myth, tale, history, chronicle of a race, or a race, I don't
    know if I speak,
and if I do speak, I don't know if I pray—to what pray?—or if I sing; do
    I dare sing?

Who would be with me? Would there be indication of household past
    the scatter of seed,
the cracked-open, gnawed-open bones there would have to have been
    to sustain me?

Cold, cold ending; rain rising and ending, ever menacing night circling
    towards me;
might I dream, at least, singing; toneless nearly, two notes or three,
    modeless, but singing?

Not yet in a garden, of morality or of mind, not yet in the shimmering
    prisms of reflection,
there must still be past the prattle and haggle of breath some aspiration
    to propel me.

A gust of upgroaning ardor, flurries of sad meditation, nostalgia for so
    much already lost:
in a stumble of uncountable syllables spun from pulse and passion some-
    thing sings, and I sing.

Grief

Dossie Williams, 1914–1995

1

Gone now, after the days of desperate, unconscious gasping, the reflexive staying alive,
tumorous lungs, tumorous blood, ruined, tumorous liver demanding to live, to go on,
even the innocent bladder, its tenuous, dull golden coin in the slack translucent bag;
gone now, after the months of scanning, medication, nausea, hair loss and weight loss;
remission, partial remission, gratitude, hope, lost hope, anxiety, anger, confusion,
the hours and days of everyday life, something like life but only as dying is like life;
gone the quiet at the end of dying, the mouth caught agape on its last bite at a breath,
bare skull with its babylike growth of new hair thrown back to open the terrified larynx;
the flesh given way but still of the world, lost but still in the world with the living;
my hand on her face, on her brow, the sphere of her skull, her arm, so thin, so wasted;
gone, yet of us and with us, a person, not yet mere dream or imagination, then, gone, wholly,
under the earth, cold earth, cold grasses, cold winter wind, freezing eternity, cold, forever.

2

Is this grief? Tears took me, then ceased; the wish to die, too, may have
    fled through me,
but not more than with any moment's despair, the old, surging wish to
    be freed, finished.
I feel pain, pain for her fear, pain for her having to know she was going,
    though we must;
pain for the pain of my daughter and son, for my wife whose despair
    for her mother returned;
pain for all human beings who know they will go and still go as though
    they knew nothing,
even pain for myself, my incomprehension, my fear of stories never
    begun now never ending.
But still, is this grief: waking too early, tiring too quickly, distracted,
    impatient, abrupt,
but still waking, still thinking and working; is this what grief is, is this
    sorrow enough?
I go to the mirror: someone who might once have felt something merely
    regards me,
eyes telling nothing, mouth saying nothing, nothing reflected but the
    things of the world,
nothing told not of any week's, no, already ten days now, any ten days'
    normal doings.
Shouldn't the face evidence anguish, shouldn't its loving sadness and
    loss be revealed?
Ineffable, vague, elusive, uncertain, distracted: shouldn't grief have a
    form of its own,
and shouldn't mind know past its moment of vague, uncertain distrac-
    tion the sureness of sorrow;

shouldn't soul flinch as we're taught proper souls are supposed to, in
reverence and fear?
Shouldn't grief be pure and complete, reshaping the world in itself, in
grief for itself?

3

Eighty, dying, in bed, tubes in her chest, my mother puts on her morn-
ing makeup;
the broad, deft strokes of foundation, the blended-in rouge, powder, eye
shadow, lipstick;
that concentration with which you must gaze at yourself, that ravenous,
unfaltering focus.
Grief for my mother, for whatever she thought her face had to be, to
be made every morning;
grief for my mother-in-law in her last declining, destroying dementia,
getting it wrong,
the thick ropes of rouge, garish green paint on her lips; mad, misplaced
slash of mascara;
grief for all women's faces, applied, created, trying to manifest what the
soul seeks to be;
grief for the faces of all human beings, our own faces telling us so much
and no more,
offering pain to all who behold them, but which when they turn to
themselves, petrify, pose.
Grief for the faces of adults who must gaze in their eyes deeply so as
not to glimpse death,
and grief for the young who see only their own relentless and grievous
longing for love.

Grief for my own eyes that try to seek truth, even of pain, of grief, but
    find only approximation.

4

My face beneath your face, face of grief, countenance of loss, of fear,
    of irrevocable extinction;
matrix laid upon matrix, mystery on mystery, guise upon guise, sem-
    blance, effigy, likeness.
Oh, to put the face of grief on in the morning; the tinting, smoothing,
    shining and shaping;
and at the end of the day, to remove it, detach it, emerge from the
    sorrowful mask.
Stripped now of its raiment, the mouth, caught in its last labored breath,
    finds last resolution;
all the flesh now, stripped of its guises, moves towards its place in the
    peace of the earth.
Grief for the earth, accepting the grief of the flesh and the grief of our
    grieving forever;
grief for the flesh and the body and face, for the eyes that can see only
    into the world,
and the mind that can only think and feel what the world gives it to
    think and to feel;
grief for the mind gone, the flesh gone, the imperfect pain that must
    stay for its moment;
and grief for the moment, its partial beauties, its imperfect affections,
    all severed, all torn.

II

Symbols

1 / WIND

Night, a wildly lashing deluge driving in great gusts over the blind,
  defeated fields,
the usually stoical larches and pines only the mewling of their suddenly
  malleable branches;
a wind like a knife that never ceased shrieking except during the stun-
  ning volleys of thunder.

By morning, half the hundred pullets in the henhouse had massed in
  a corner and smothered,
an inert, intricate structure of dulled iridescence and still-distracted, still-
  frenzied eyes,
the vivid sapphire of daybreak tainted by a vaporous, gorge-swelling fetor.

The tribe of survivors compulsively hammered their angular faces as
  usual into the trough:
nothing in the world, they were saying, not carnage or dissolution, can
  bear reflection;
the simplest acts of being, they were saying, can obliterate all, all mad-
  ness, all mourning.

2 / GUITAR

For long decades the guitar lay disregarded in its case, unplucked and
   untuned,
then one winter morning, the steam heat coming on hard, the maple
   neck swelling again,
the sixth, gravest string, weary of feeling itself submissively tugged to and
   fro

over the ivory lip of the bridge, could no longer bear the tension pre-
   ceding release,
and, with a faint thud and a single, weak note like a groan stifled in a
   fist, it gave way,
its portions curling agonizingly back on themselves like sundered seg-
   ments of worm.

. . . The echoes abruptly decay; silence again, the other strings still
   steadfast, still persevering,
still feeling the music potent within them, their conviction of timeless-
   ness only confirmed,
of being essential, elemental, like earth, fire, air, from which all beauty
   must be evolved.

3 / OWL

The just-fledged baby owl a waiter has captured under a tree near the
      island restaurant
seems strangely unfazed to be on display on a formica table, though she
      tilts ludicrously,
all her weight on one leg as though she had merely paused in her lift
      towards departure.

Immobile except for her constantly swivelling head, she unpredictably
      fixes her gaze,
clicking from one far focus to another—sea, tree, sky, sometimes it seems
      even star—
but never on hand or eye, no matter how all in the circle around her
      chirp and cajole.

Thus the gods once, thus still perhaps gods: that scrutiny densely grained
      as granite,
the rotation calibrated on chromium bearings; dilation, contraction;
      wrath, disdain and remove . . .
But oh, to be slipping ever backwards in time, the savage memories, the
      withheld cry!

4 / DOG

Howl after pitiful, aching howl: an enormous, efficiently muscular dob-
     erman pinscher
has trapped itself in an old-fashioned phone booth, the door closed
     firmly upon it,
but when someone approaches to try to release it, the howl quickens
     and descends,

and if someone in pity dares anyway lean on and crack open an inch
     the obstinate hinge,
the quickened howl is a snarl, the snarl a blade lathed in the scarlet
     gape of the gullet,
and the creature powers itself towards that sinister slit, ears flattened,
     fangs flashing,

the way, caught in the deepest, most unknowing cell of itself, heart's
     secret, heart's wound,
decorous usually, seemly, though starving now, desperate, will turn
     nonetheless, raging,
ready to kill, or die, to stay where it is, to maintain itself just as it is,
     decorous, seemly.

5 / FIRE

The plaster had been burnt from the studs, the two-by-four joists were
      eaten with char;
ceilings smoke-blackened, glass fragments and foul, soaked rags of old
      rug underfoot:
even the paint on the outside brick had bubbled in scabs and blisters
      and melted away.

Though the fire was ostensibly out, smoke still drifted up through cracks
      in the floor,
and sometimes a windowsill or a door frame would erupt in pale, insid-
      ious flames,
subtle in the darkness, their malignancies masked in blushes of tem-
      perate violet and rose.

Like love it was, love ill and soiled; like affection, affinity, passion, mis-
      used and consumed;
warmth betrayed, patience exhausted, distorted, all evidence of kindness
      now unkindness . . .
Yet still the hulk, the gutted carcass; fuming ash and ember; misery and
      shame.

6 / DAWN

Herds of goats puttering by on the rock-strewn path in what sounded
      like felt slippers;
before that (because the sudden awareness of it in sleep always came
      only after it passed),
the church-bell, its cry in the silence like a swell of loneliness, then
      loneliness healed.

The resonant *clock* of the fisherman's skiff being tethered to the end of
      the jetty;
the sad, repetitive smack of a catch of squid being slapped onto a slab
      of concrete;
the waves, their eternal morning torpor, the cypress leaning warily back
      from the shore.

A voice from a hill or another valley, expanding, concretizing like light,
      falling, fading,
then a comic grace-note, the creak of rickety springs as someone turns
      in their bed:
so much beginning, and now, sadness nearly, to think one might not
      even have known!

7 / WIG

The bus that won't arrive this freezing, bleak, pre-Sabbath afternoon
  must be Messiah;
the bewigged woman, pacing the sidewalk, furious, seething, can be only
  the mystic Shekinah,
the presence of God torn from Godhead, chagrined, abandoned, long-
  ing to rejoin, reunite.

The husband in his beard and black hat, pushing a stroller a step behind
  her as she stalks?
The human spirit, which must slog through such degrading tracts of
  slush and street-filth,
bound forever to its other, no matter how incensed she may be, how
  obliviously self-absorbed.

And the child, asleep, serene, uncaring in the crank and roar of traffic,
  his cheeks afire,
ladders of snowy light leaping and swirling above him, is what else but
  psyche, holy psyche,
always only now just born, always now just waking, to the ancient truths
  of knowledge, suffering, loss.

8 / GARDEN

A garden I usually never would visit; oaks, roses, the scent of roses I
    usually wouldn't remark
but do now, in a moment for no reason suddenly unlike any other,
    numinous, limpid, abundant,
whose serenity lifts and enfolds me, as a swirl of breeze lifts the leaves
    and enfolds them.

Nothing ever like this, not even love, though there's no need to measure,
    no need to compare:
for once not to be waiting, to be in the world as time moves through
    and across me,
to exult in this fragrant light given to me, in this flow of warmth given
    to me and the world.

Then, on my hand beside me on the bench, something, I thought some-
    body else's hand, alighted;
I flinched it off, and saw—sorrow!—a warbler, grey, black, yellow, in
    flight already away.
It stopped near me in a shrub, though, and waited, as though unstartled,
    as though unafraid,

as though to tell me my reflex of fear was no failure, that if I believed
    I had lost something,
I was wrong, because nothing can be lost, of the self, of a lifetime of
    bringing forth selves.
Then it was gone, its branch springing back empty: still oak, though,
    still rose, still world.

III

_____

Realms

Often I have thought that after my death, not in death's void as we
      usually think it,
but in some simpler after-realm of the mind, it will be given to me to
      transport myself
through all space and all history, to behold whatever and converse with
      whomever I wish.

Sometimes I might be an actual presence, a traveller listening at the
      edge of the crowd;
at other times I'd have no physical being; I'd move unseen but seeing
      through palace or slum.
Sophocles, Shakespeare, Bach! Grandfathers! Homo-erectus! The uni-
      verse bursting into being!

Now, though, as I wake, caught by some imprecise longing, you in the
      darkness beside me,
your warmth flowing gently against me, it comes to me that in all my
      after-death doings,
I see myself as alone, always alone, and I'm suddenly stranded, forsaken,
      desperate, lost.

To propel myself through those limitless reaches without you! Never!
      Be with me, come!
Babylon, Egypt, Lascaux, the new seas boiling up life; Dante, Delphi,
      Magyars and Mayans!
Wait, though, it must be actually you, not my imagination of you, how-
      ever real: for myself,

45

mind would suffice, no matter if all were one of time's terrible toys, but
    I must have you,
as you are, the unquenchable fire of your presence, otherwise death
    truly would triumph.
Quickly, never mind death, never mind mute, oblivious, onrushing
    time: wake, hold me!

Storm

Another burst of the interminable, intermittently torrential dark after-
    noon downpour,
and the dozens of tirelessly garrulous courtyard sparrows stop hectoring
    each other
and rush to park under a length of cornice endearingly soiled with
    decades of wing-grease.

The worst summer in memory, thermal inversion, smog, swelter, inti-
    mations of global warming;
though the plane trees still thrust forth buds as though innocent April
    were just blooming,
last week's tentative pre-green leaflings are already woefully charred with
    heat and pollution.

Thunder far off, benign, then closer, slashes of lightning, a massive,
    concussive unscrolling,
an answering tremor in the breast, the exaltation at sharing a planet with
    this, then sorrow,
that we really might strip it of all but the bare wounded rock lumbering
    down its rote rail.

A denser veil of clouds now, another darkening downlash, the wind rises,
    the sparrows scatter,
the leaves quake, and Oh, I throw myself this way, the trees say, then
    that way, I tremble,
I moan, and still you don't understand the absence I'll be in the void
    of unredeemable time.

. . . Twelve suns, the prophecies promise, twelve vast suns of purification
    will mount the horizon,

to scorch, sear, burn away, then twelve cosmic cycles of rain: no tree
    left, no birdsong,
only the vigilant, acid waves, vindictively scouring themselves again and
    again on no shore.

Imagine then the emergence: Oh, this way, the sky streaked, Oh, that
    way, with miraculous brightness;
imagine us, beginning again, timid and tender, with a million years
    more this time to evolve,
an epoch more on all fours, stricken with shame and repentance, before
    we fire our forges.

Song

A city square, paths empty, sky clear; after days of rain, a purified sun-
  light blazed through;
all bright, all cool, rinsed shadows all vivid; the still-dripping leaves sated
  prolific.

Suddenly others: voices, anger; sentences started, aborted; harsh, honed
  hisses of fury:
two adults, a child, the grown-ups raging, the child, a girl, seven or
  eight, wide-eyed, distracted.

"You, you," the parents boiled on in their clearly eternal battle: "you
  creature, you cruel,"
and the child stood waiting, instead of going to play on the slide or the
  swing, stood listening.

I wished she would weep; I could imagine the rich, abashing gush
  springing from her:
otherwise mightn't she harden her heart; mightn't she otherwise without
  knowing it become scar?

But the day was still perfect, the child, despite her evident apprehension,
  slender, exquisite:
when she noticed me watching, she precociously, flirtily, fetchingly
  swept back her hair.

Yes, we know one another, yes, there in the sad broken music of mind
  where nothing is lost.
Sorrow, love, they were so sweetly singing: *where shall I refuge seek if
  you refuse me?*

Insight

1

All under the supposition that he's helping her because she's so often
    melancholy lately,
he's pointing out certain problems with her character, but he's so seri-
    ous, so vehement,
she realizes he's *attacking* her, to hurt, not help; she doesn't know what
    might be driving him,
but she finds she's thinking through his life for him, the losses, the long-
    forgotten sadnesses,
and though she can't come up with anything to correlate with how
    hatefully he's acting,
she thinks *something* has to be there, so she listens, nods, sometimes she
    actually agrees.

2

They're only arguing, but all at once she feels anxiety, and realizes she's
    afraid of him,
then, wondering whether she should risk expressing it to him, she un-
    derstands she can't,
that the way he is these days he'll turn it back on her, and so she keeps
    it to herself,
then, despite herself, she wonders what their life's become to have to
    hide so much,
then comes a wave of disappointment, with herself, not him, and not
    for that initial fear,
but for some cowardice, some deeper dread that makes her ask, why not
    him?

3

He's very distant, but when she asks him what it is, he insists it's nothing,
  though it's not,
she knows it's not, because he never seems to face her and his eyes
  won't hold on hers;
it makes her feel uncertain, clumsy, then as though she's somehow sup-
  plicating him:
though she wants nothing more from him than she already has—what
  would he think she'd want?—
when she tries to trust him, to believe his offhanded reassurance, she
  feels that she's pretending,
it's like a game, though very serious, like trying to talk yourself out of
  an imminent illness.

4

If there are sides to take, he'll take the other side, against anything she
  says, to anyone:
at first she thinks it's just coincidence; after all, she knows she's some-
  times wrong,
everyone is sometimes wrong, but with him now all there seem to be
  are sides, she's always wrong;
even when she doesn't know she's arguing, when she doesn't care, he
  finds her wrong,
in herself it seems she's wrong, she feels she should apologize, to some-
  one, anyone, to him;
him, him, him; what is it that he wants from her: remorse, contrition,
  should she just *die?*

5

He's telling her in much too intricate detail about a film he's seen: she
     tries to change the subject,
he won't let her, and she finds she's questioning herself—must she be
     so critical, judgmental?—
then she's struck, from something in his tone, or absent from his tone,
     some lack of resonance,
that why he's going on about the movie is because there's nothing else
     to say to her,
or, worse, that there are things to say but not to her, they're too intimate
     to waste on her:
it's *she*, she thinks, who's being measured and found wanting, and what
     should she think now?

6

This time her, her story, about something nearly noble she once did, a
     friend in trouble,
and she helped, but before she's hardly started he's made clear he thinks
     it's all a fantasy,
and she as quickly understands that what he really means is that her
     love, her love for him,
should reflexively surpass the way she loved, or claims she loved, the
     long-forgotten friend,
and with a shock of sorrow, she knows she can't tell him that, that the
     betrayal,
and certainly there is one, isn't his desire to wound, but her thinking
     that he shouldn't.

7

She sits in his lap, she's feeling lonely, nothing serious, she just wants
       sympathy, company,
then she realizes that though she hasn't said a word, he's sensed her
       sadness and is irked,
feels that she's inflicting, as she always does, he seems to think, her
       misery on him,
so she tells herself not to be so needy anymore, for now, though, she
       just wants to leave,
except she can't, she knows that if he suspects he's let her down he'll
       be more irritated still,
and so she stays, feeling dumb and out of place, and heavy, heavier, like
       a load of stone.

8

She experiences a pleasurable wave of nostalgia, not for her own past,
       but for his:
she can sense and taste the volume and the textures of the room he
       slept in as a child,
until she reminds herself she's never been there, never even seen the
       place, so, reluctantly,
she thinks reluctantly, she wonders if she might not be too close, too
       devoted to him,
whether she might actually be trying to become him, then she feels
       herself resolve, to her surprise,
to disengage from him, and such a sense of tiredness takes her that she
       almost cries.

9

As usual these days he's angry with her, and because she wants him not
     to be she kisses him,
but perhaps because he's so surprised, she feels him feel her kiss came
     from some counter-anger,
then she starts to doubt herself, wondering if she might have meant it
     as he thinks she did,
as a traitor kiss, a Judas kiss, and if that's true, his anger, both his angers,
     would be justified:
look, though, how he looks at her, with bemusement, hardly hidden,
     he knows her so well,
he senses her perplexity, her swell of guilt and doubt: how he cherishes
     his wrath!

10

Such matters end, there are healings, breakings-free; she tells herself
     they end, but still,
years later, when the call she'd dreaded comes, when he calls, asking
     why she hasn't called,
as though all those years it wasn't her who'd called, then stopped calling
     and began to wait,
then stopped waiting, healed, broke free, so when he innocently suggests
     they get together,
she says absolutely not, but feels uncertain—is she being spiteful?
     small?—and then she knows:
after this he'll cause her no more pain, though no matter how she
     wished it weren't, this is pain.

In Darkness

That old documentary about the miners' strike in Harlan County, the
    company hireling, the goon,
who's brought in as a guard for the scabs and ends up blowing a miner's
    brains out:
how he, the thug, the enforcer, confronting the strikers, facing them
    down, pistol in hand,
ready to kill, maim, slaughter, destroy, evidences no compunction, no
    trepidation, no fear,
and you know it's because he has no reverence for creaturely existence,
    even his own,
to deflect him from what for him are the only true issues, obedience,
    wealth, property, power;
how he posed, strutted, snarled in contempt at those he conceived were
    beneath him,
the way, now, so many in power, assuming that same stance of righteous
    rectitude and rage,
snarl their contempt at those who'd dare hold differing notions of gov-
    ernance and justice.

And when, after, the strikers met in the bare, scrufty yard of their dead
    friend's house,
and found there in the dust a shining shard, an arch of perfectly white
    human skull-bone;
though it was midnight, with just enough faint moonlight to make out
    the circle of faces,
you could see that despite their resolve they were frightened, despite
    their desperate need
they were awed at having to know once again how brief our mortal
    moment of time is,

while behind them, the thug, the enforcer, prowled and raved, teeth
    clenched, jaw grinding,
his ravenous craving for order unslaked, his fear and his longing for love
    extracted forever,
as now, they, the political thugs, crazed with power, prowl, waiting to
    wreak social mayhem,
not for charity's sake but submission's, not for compassion but for ap-
    peasement of limitless greed.

The Demagogue

As on the rim of a cup crusted with rancid honey a host of hornets
      suddenly settles,
congealing in a mindless, ravenous mass, bristling with stingers of men-
      ace and rage, thus they,

so muddled with the rich intoxicant bliss of his resentment they forget
      who they are,
congregate, mass, swarm on his lips, to suck at his sanctimonious syrups
      of indignation,

that which once was love in them so corrupted that when he urges
      them—warriors, hornets—
to lift the cup of spiritual violence to their lips and drink, they do lift,
      they do drink.

The Bed

Beds squalling, squealing, muffled in hush; beds pitching, leaping, im-
mobile as mountains;
beds wide as a prairie, strait as a gate, as narrow as the plank of a ship
to be walked.

*I squalled, I squealed, I swooped and pitched; I covered my eyes and fell
from the plank.*

Beds proud, beds preening, beds timid and tense; vanquished beds wish-
ing only to vanquish;
neat little beds barely scented and dented, beds so disused you cranked
them to start them.

*I admired, sang praises, flattered, adored; I sighed and submitted, solaced,
comforted, cranked.*

Procrustean beds with consciences sharpened like razors slicing the
darkness above you;
beds like the labors of Hercules, stables and serpents; Samson blinded,
Noah in horror.

*Blind with desire, I wakened in horror, in toil, in bondage, my conscience
in tatters.*

Beds sobbing, beds sorry, beds pleading, beds mournful with histories
that amplified yours,
so you knelled through their dolorous echoes as through the depths of
your own dementias.

I echoed, I knelled, I sobbed and repented, I bandaged the wrists, sighed
  for embryos lost.

A nation of beds, a cosmos, then, how could it still happen, the bed at
  the end of the world,
as welcoming as the world, ark, fortress, light and delight, the other beds
  all forgiven, forgiving.

A bed that sang through the darkness and woke in song as though world
  itself had just wakened;
two beds fitted together as one; bed of peace, patience, arrival, bed of
  unwaning ardor.

The Heart

When I saw my son's heart blown up in bland black and white on the
      sonogram screen,
an amoebic, jellylike mass barely contained by invisible layers of
      membrane, I felt faint.

Eight years old, Jed lay, apparently unafraid, wires strung from him into
      the clicking machine,
as the doctor showed us a pliable, silvery lid he explained was the valve,
      benignly prolapsed,

which to me looked like some lost lunar creature biting too avidly,
      urgently at an alien air,
the tiniest part of that essence I'd always allowed myself to believe could
      stand for the soul.

Revealed now in a nakedness nearly not to be looked upon as the mus-
      cular ghost of itself,
it majestically swelled and contracted, while I stood trembling before it,
      in love, in dread.

Exterior: Day

Two actors are awkwardly muscling a coffin out of a doorway draped in
 black funeral hangings;
a third sobs, unconvincingly, though: the director cries "Cut!" and they
 set up again.

Just then an old woman, blind, turns the corner; guiding herself down
 the side of the building,
she touches the velvet awning and visibly startles: has someone died and
 she not been told?

You can almost see her in her mind move through the entrance, and
 feel her way up the stairs,
knocking, trying doors—who might be missing?—but out here every-
 thing holds.

For a long moment no one knows what to do: the actors fidget, the
 cameraman looks away;
the woman must be aware that the street is unnaturally quiet, but she
 still doesn't move.

It begins to seem like a contest, an agon; illusion and truth: crew, on-
 lookers, and woman;
her hand still raised, caught in the cloth, her vast, uninhabited gaze
 sweeping across us.

Time: 1978

1

What could be more endearing, on a long, too quiet, lonely evening in
    an unfamiliar house,
than, on the table before us, Jed's sneakers, which, finally, at eleven
    o'clock, I notice,
tipped on their sides, still tied, the soles barely scuffed since we just
    bought them today,
or rather submitted to Jed's picking them out, to his absolutely having
    to have them,
the least practical pair, but the first thing besides toys he's ever cared so
    much about,
and which, despite their impossible laces and horrible color, he pas-
    sionately wanted, *desired*,
and coerced us into buying, by, when we made him try on the sensible
    pair we'd chosen,
limping in them, face twisted in torment: his first anguished ordeal of
    a violated aesthetic.

2

What more endearing except Jed himself, who, now, perhaps because
    of the new night noises,
wakes, and, not saying a word, pads in to sit on Catherine's lap, head
    on her breast, silent,
only his breathing, sleep-quickened, as I write this, trying to get it all
    in, hold the moments
between the sad desolation I thought if not to avert then to diminish in
    writing it down,

and this, now, my pen scratching, eyes rushing to follow the line and
    not lose Jed's gaze,
which dims with sleep now, wanders to the window—hills, brush, field
    cleft with trenches—
and begins to flutter so that I can't keep up with it: quick, quick, before
    you're asleep,
listen, how and whenever if not now, now, will I speak to you, both of
    you, of all this?

Hawk

Whatever poison it had ingested or injury incurred had flung it in agony
      onto its back,
and it drove itself with shuddering, impotent flails of its wings into the
      dirt.

When it stopped, I came closer, thinking its sufferings over, but it sav-
      agely started again,
talons retracted, spine cramped grotesquely, pinions beginning to shatter
      and fray.

I knew what to do, but, child of the city, I couldn't: there was no one
      to help me;
I could only—forgive me—retreat from that frantic, irrational thrashing,
      thinking as I went,

Die, please, the way, it came to me with a startling remorse, I did when
      my father was dying,
when he woke from the probe in his brain to the worse than death
      waiting for him.

There'd be long moments he'd seem not to breathe: absolute stillness,
      four long beats, more,
between huge inhalations, and, Go, I'd think, *die, be released from the
      toil of your dying.*

I'd think it again and again, with the fierce anguished impatience of
      the child I was now again,
then I'd wonder: might this be only my unpardonably wanting my own
      anxiety to be over?

When at last he'd open his eyes, I'd think, *No, stay, be with us as long
    as you can,*
relieved I at least could think that; but that other shock of misgiving
    still holds me.

I was frightened, then, too; then, too, something was asked and I wasn't
    who I wanted to be.
How seldom I am, how much more often this self-sundering doubt, this
    bewildering contending.

The Lover

for Michel Rétiveau

Maybe she missed the wife, or the wife's better dinner parties, but she
    never forgave him,
the lover, not for having caused the husband to switch gender prefer-
    ence, but for being,
she must have said, or sighed, a thousand times, so difficult to be with,
    so crude, so *tiresome*.

But it was she who began to bore, the way she kept obsessively ques-
    tioning his legitimacy—
so *arch* he was, she'd say, so *bitchy*—and all after the rest of us had
    come to appreciate
his mildly sardonic, often brilliant bantering, his casual erudition in so
    many arcane areas.

It's true that at first he may have seemed at least a little of what she said
    he was—
obstreperously, argumentatively, if wittily, abrasive—but we assigned that
    to what,
considering the pack of friends' old friends with which he was faced,
    was a reasonable apprehension

about being received into a society so elaborate in the intricacies of its
    never articulated
but still forbiddingly solidified rituals of acceptance: he really handled
    it quite graciously.
What after all did she expect of him? Shyness? Diffidence? The diffi-
    dence of what? A bride?

The Game

"Water" was her answer and I fell instantly and I knew self-destructively
      in love with her,
had to have her, would, I knew, someday, I didn't care how, and soon,
      too, have her,
though I guessed already it would have to end badly though not so
      disastrously as it did.

My answer, "lion" or "eagle," wasn't important: the truth would have
      been anything but myself.
The game of that first fateful evening was what you'd want to come back
      as after you died;
it wasn't the last life-or-death contest we'd have, only the least erotically
      driven and dangerous.

What difference if she was married, and perhaps mad (both only a little,
      I thought wrongly)?
There was only my jealous glimpse of her genius, then my vision of
      vengeance: midnight, morning—
beneath me a planet possessed: cycles of transfiguration and soaring,
      storms crossing.

Spider Psyche

The mummified spider hung in its own web in the rafters striped legs
    coiled tightly
into its body head hunched a bit into what would be shoulders if it had
    been human
indicating a knowledge perhaps of the death coming to take it indicating
    not fear of death
I surmise but an emotion like wanting to be ready or ready on time
    trying to prepare psyche
for death so psyche won't fall back into the now useless brain the core
    imprinted with all
it knew in the world until now but only a nub now no longer receptor
    receptacle rather
and perhaps psyche did it didn't flinch rather just gazed out of the web
    of perception
watching the wave of not-here take the shore-edge of here acknowledg-
    ing rather its portion
of being the blare of light in the corner the grain in the wood the old
    odors and the space
a great cup underneath a great gaping under the breadth of your being
    so that you want
no matter what this last moment of holding even if shoulders and brain
    can hardly abide it
even if brain swoons nearly trying to hold its last thought last fusion of
    will and cognition
and there is no end in this ending no contingent condition of being
    this glare of perception
hurl of sensation all one sense and intention act and love my psyche
    my spider love and hope
take us dear spider of self into your otherness into having once been
    and the knowledge of having

in all this been once in wonder so every instant was thanks and all else
       was beneath and adrift
my spider psyche all awe now all we ever wanted to be now in this great
       gratitude gone

Grace

Almost as good as her passion, I'll think, almost as good as her presence,
    her physical grace,
almost as good as making love with her, I'll think in my last aching
    breath before last,
my glimpse before last of the light, were her good will and good wit,
    the steadiness of her affections.

Almost, I'll think, sliding away on my sleigh of departure, the rind of
    my consciousness thinning,
the fear of losing myself, of—worse—losing her, subsiding as I think,
    hope it must,
almost as good as her beauty, her glow, was the music of her thought,
    her voice and laughter.

Almost as good as kissing her, being kissed back, I hope I'll have strength
    still to think,
was watching her as she worked or read, was beholding her selfless
    sympathy for son, friend, sister,
even was feeling her anger, sometimes, rarely, lift against me, then be
    forgotten, put aside.

Almost, I'll think, as good as our unlikely coming together, was our
    constant, mostly unspoken debate
as to whether good in the world was good in itself, or (my side) only
    the absence of evil:
no need to say how much how we lived was shaped by her bright spirit,
    her humor and hope.

Almost as good as living at all—improbable gift—was watching her once
    cross our room,

the reflections of night rain she'd risen to close the window against
    flaring across her,
doubling her light, then feeling her come back to bed, reaching to find
    and embrace me,

as I'll hope she'll be there to embrace me as I sail away on that last
    voyage out of myself,
that last, sorrowful passage out of her presence, though her presence,
    I'll think, will endure,
as firmly as ever, as good even now, I'll think in that lull before last,
    almost as ever.

Time: 1972

As a child, in the half-dark, as you wait on the edge of her bed for her
     to sleep,
will lift her hand to your face and move it over your brow, cheeks, the
     orbits of your eyes,
as though she'd never quite seen you before, or really remarked you, or
     never like this,
and you're taken for a time out of your own world into hers, her world
     of new wonder,
and are touched by her wonder, her frank, forthright apprehending,
     gentle and knowing,
somehow already knowing, creating itself—you can feel it—in this out-
     flow of bestowal,

so, sometimes, in the sometimes somber halls of memory, your life as
     you've known it,
in the only way you can know it, in these disparate, unpredictable
     upsurges of mind,
gathers itself, gathers what seem like the minds behind mind that shim-
     mer within mind,
and turns back on itself, suspending itself, caught in the marvel of
     memory and time,
and, as the child's mind, so long ago now, engendered itself in attach-
     ment's touch and bestowal,
life itself now seems engendered from so much enduring attachment,
     so much bestowal.

Villanelle of the Suicide's Mother

Sometimes I almost go hours without crying,
Then I feel if I don't, I'll go insane.
It can seem her whole life was her dying.

She tried so hard, then she was tired of trying;
Now I'm tired, too, of trying to explain.
Sometimes I almost go hours without crying.

The anxiety, the rage, the denying;
Though I never blamed her for my pain,
It can seem her whole life was her dying,

And mine was struggling to save her: prying,
Conniving: it was the chemistry in her brain.
Sometimes I almost go hours without crying.

If I said she was easy, I'd be lying;
The lens between her and the world was stained:
It can seem her whole life was her dying

But the fact, the *fact*, is stupefying:
Her absence tears at me like a chain.
Sometimes I almost go hours without crying.
It can seem her whole life was her dying.

Thirst

Here was my relation with the woman who lived all last autumn and
  winter day and night
on a bench in the Hundred and Third Street subway station until finally
  one day she vanished:

we regarded each other, scrutinized one another: me shyly, obliquely,
  trying not to be furtive;
she boldly, unblinkingly, even pugnaciously; wrathfully even, when her
  bottle was empty.

I was frightened of her, I felt like a child, I was afraid some repressed
  part of myself
would go out of control and I'd be forever entrapped in the shocking
  seethe of her stench.

Not excrement, merely, not merely surface and orifice going unwashed,
  rediffusion of rum:
there was will in it, and intention, power and purpose; a social, ethical
  rage and rebellion.

. . . Despair, too, though, grief, loss: sometimes I'd think I should take
  her home with me,
bathe her, comfort her, dress her: she wouldn't have wanted me to, I
  would think.

Instead I'd step into my train: how rich, I would think, is the lexicon of
  our self-absolving;
how enduring our bland, fatal assurance that reflection is righteousness
  being accomplished.

The dance of our glances, the clash; pulling each other through our
    perceptual punctures;
then holocaust, holocaust: host on host of ill, injured presences squan-
    dered, consumed.

Her vigil, somewhere, I know, continues: her occupancy, her absolute,
    faithful attendance;
the dance of our glances: challenge, abdication, effacement; the per-
    fume of our consternation.

Old Man

Special: Big Tits, says the advertisement for a soft-core magazine on our
    neighborhood newsstand,
but forget her breasts—a lush, fresh-lipped blonde, skin glowing gold,
    sprawls there, resplendent.
Sixty nearly, yet these hardly tangible, hardly better than harlots can still
    stir me.

Maybe coming of age in the American sensual darkness, never seeing
    an unsmudged nipple,
an uncensored vagina, has left me forever infected with an unquench-
    able lust of the eye:
always that erotic murmur—I'm hardly myself if I'm not in a state of
    incipient desire.

God knows, though, there are worse twists your obsessions can take: last
    year, in Israel,
a young ultra-Orthodox rabbi, guiding some teen-aged girls through the
    shrine of the *Shoah,*
forbade them to look in one room because there were images in it he
    said were licentious.

The display was a photo: men and women, stripped naked, some trying
    to cover their genitals,
others too frightened to bother, lined up in snow waiting to be shot and
    thrown in a ditch.
The girls to my horror averted their gaze: what carnal mistrust had their
    teacher taught them?

Even that, though . . . Another confession: once, in a book on pre-war
    Poland, a studio-portrait,

an absolute angel, with tormented, tormenting eyes; I kept finding my-
    self at her page;
that she died in the camps made her, I didn't dare wonder why, more
    present, more precious.

"Died in the camps": that, too, people, or Jews anyway, kept from their
    children back then,
but it was like sex, you didn't have to be told. Sex and death: how close
    they can seem.
So constantly conscious now of death moving towards me, sometimes I
    think I confound them.

My wife's loveliness almost consumes me, my passion for her goes be-
    yond reasonable bounds;
when we make love, her holding me, everywhere all around me, I'm
    there and not there,
my mind teems, jumbles of faces, voices, impressions: I live my life over
    as though I were drowning.

. . . Then I am drowning, in despair, at having to leave her, this, every-
    thing, all: unbearable, awful . . .
Still, to be able to die with no special contrition, not having been slaugh-
    tered or enslaved,
and not having to know history's next mad rage or regression—it might
    be a relief.

No, again no, I don't mean that for a moment, what I mean is the world
    holds me so tightly,
the good and the bad, my own follies and weakness, that even this
    counterfeit Venus,

with her sham heat and her bosom probably plumped with gel, so moves
    me my breath catches.

Vamp, siren, seductress, how much more she reveals in her glare of ink
    than she knows;
how she incarnates our desperate human need for regard, our passion
    to live in beauty,
to be beauty, to be cherished, by glances if by no more, of something
    like love, or love.